MW00424817

*Presented to*

_____

*By*

_____

*Date*

_____

# BREATH
# PRAYERS

*Simple Whispers That Keep You in God's Presence*

**HONOR HB BOOKS**

*Inspiration and Motivation for the Seasons of Life*

COOK COMMUNICATIONS MINISTRIES
Colorado Springs, Colorado • Paris, Ontario
KINGSWAY COMMUNICATIONS LTD
Eastbourne, England

Honor Books® is an imprint of
Cook Communications Ministries, Colorado Springs, CO 80918
Cook Communications, Paris, Ontario
Kingsway Communications Ltd, Eastbourne, England

BREATH PRAYERS—SIMPLE WHISPERS THAT KEEP YOU IN GOD'S
PRESENCE
© 2004 by BORDON BOOKS
6532 East 71st St, Suite 105
Tulsa, OK 74133

Printed in the United States of America.
2  3  4  5  6  Printing/Year  08  07  06  05  04

Compiled and written by Melissa Killian, Killian Creative
Cover designed by LJ Designs
Developed by Bordon Books

ISBN 1-56292-231-9

# WHAT IS A BREATH PRAYER?

Even if you spend time in the morning with God, by the time you've finished item number ten on your list of things to do, the peace you felt may have evaporated; and perhaps He feels very far away. But He is as close as your breath; and you can spend your entire day with Him—even on the run. Breath prayers are brief, heartfelt prayers that can help you enjoy God's company and surround your loved ones with prayer without retreating to the mountains and giving up your to-do list. The secret is a short prayer that you whisper to God as you go about the business of your day, allowing your experiences to prompt you. As you see a friend, you can pray, "Father, bless her." As you stand in line, you can pray "Father, bless her" for the cashier as someone argues with her. When you get to that three o'clock slump and wonder how you are going to get everything done, you can pray, "Father, bless me."

Instead of leaving God in the corner with your Bible, breath prayers can help you to live a life in which God walks with you daily as you talk to Him about the things that cross your path. Your life will be transformed as you live continually in God's presence.

Best of all is it to preserve
everything in a pure, still heart,
and let there be for every
pulse a thanksgiving,
and for every breath a song.

KONRAD VON GESNER


*Pray without ceasing.*

1 THESSALONIANS 5:17 NKJV

# How to Use *Breath Prayers*

After you have read **Breath Prayers,** choose a suitable prayer to use throughout your day. Repeat it so that you can say it to yourself in one breath, both in and out. Each breath is a prayer. In this way you will pray without ceasing, aware of God walking through each experience with you.

As you see people or think of them, as you experience situations or feelings, offer that prayer to God. "I exalt You, Lord," can become the refrain of your heart when you see drivers around you on the road and as you see various people. "I exalt You, Lord," can mean you celebrate with God others' existence. It can mean you celebrate God's Lordship and loving care of them. It can also mean you praise God even though things are not going your way at the moment. The words will stay the same, but each breath you pray will be unique in the way you mean it to God. And you will maintain a constant connection with Him.

*[Pray] always with all prayer and
supplication in the Spirit, being watchful
to this end with all perseverance
and supplication for all the saints.*

EPHESIANS 6:18 NKJV

# I CAN DO ALL THINGS THROUGH YOU, LORD.

*I can do everything through him
who gives me strength.*

PHILIPPIANS 4:13 NIV

"I can't" or "I'll never" are words that echo
through all our minds at times. Self-doubt might
be keeping you from accomplishing all that God
has for you to do. How often have you felt
"unable" to pursue a dream that keeps tugging
at your heart, maybe even keeping you awake at
night? You may find yourself continually feeling
dissatisfied with the status quo.

Fortunately, those who put their hope in
Christ can rely on God's promises. He assures us
that all things are possible to those who believe;

8

that we can do all things through Christ who gives us strength—especially where we are weak. If God is for you, who can prevail against you? He will help you to accomplish the things He has put in your heart to do.

I can pray a breath prayer, *I can do all things through You, Lord*, when—

- I feel weak or afraid.

- I'm not sure what to do.

- I lack confidence in my skills.

- others tell me I'm not good enough.

- someone else seems more talented than me.

**I can do all things through You, Lord.**

# TEACH ME YOUR WAY.

*Show me your ways, O Lord,*
*teach me your paths;*
*guide me in your truth and teach me.*

PSALMS 25:4-5 NIV

How do we know when to stand firm in a situation, or when to let go? Learning to discern God's will is the most challenging call we have as Christians. Often we feel at a loss about how to follow the Lord's leading—or worse, that we've already missed it. What does the Lord require of us as Christians anyway?

In 2 Peter 1:3 we are told that God has provided all things pertaining to life and godliness in order that we might partake of His own divine nature. We are told to follow after peace, to be led by love, and to be lovers of the truth. Micah sums up what the Lord requires

as this: to act justly, love mercy, and walk
humbly with our God. (See Micah 6:8.) This is
all we need to do as we strive to please God.

I can pray a breath prayer, *Teach me Your way*,
when—

- circumstances tempt me do something
  not quite right.

- I don't know how to respond to
  someone.

- others draw me into an uncomfortable
  situation.

- I'm not sure which option is right.

- everything before me seems wrong, and
  I need an inspired alternative.

**Teach me Your way.**

# UNITE MY HEART.

*Give me an undivided heart,*
*that I may fear your name.*

PSALMS 86:11 NIV

Divided mind. Divided heart. Divided tongue. We have all fallen prey to either our own double-mindedness, or what we sometimes call a "two-faced" colleague or relative. We know from the letter of James that "a double-minded man is unstable in all his ways" and will not receive any thing from the Lord (James 1:7-8 KJV).

David cries out throughout the Psalms for God to unite his heart to fear the Lord; and we know from Proverbs that the fear of the Lord is the beginning of wisdom. The Israelites were commanded to worship God with their whole heart, mind, and strength. In today's "divided world," we must keep our hearts from being divided if we are to be in a position to help others. We must love and fear God with all our heart— our whole heart—and not just a convenient portion of it.

I can pray a breath prayer, *Unite my heart,* when—

- setting priorities.

- other people draw me into "derogatory" humor.

- making time and financial management decisions.

- deciding what to watch on TV.

- my children are listening.

**Unite my heart.**

# GIVE ME YOUR WORDS.

*"The Lord GOD has given Me
the tongue of the learned,
that I should know how to speak
a word in season to him who is weary.*

ISAIAH 50:4 NKJV

Maybe it's a Friday, and you are filling in at
the church office. You're in a hurry. Nothing has
gone right all day. A woman comes into the
reception area looking for financial help. She
asks if you could help her out with some grocery
certificates or a gas voucher. "No, we don't have
any today. Sorry," you say, wanting to get back
to work. She asks if you know where else she
might go for help. "No," you say. You don't
have any idea. You want to finish your work so
you can leave on time.

She walks out the door and you stand there

for several long moments gazing after her, your heart sinking at the missed opportunity. "What could I have done?" you think to yourself. The answers rise up in your spirit—you could have prayed with her, given her an encouraging word, pointed her to the Provider of all things. Yes, you did know where else she could turn for help. Peter's words ring in your ears, "Always be prepared to give an answer to everyone who asks you to give the reason for the hope that you have" (1 Peter 3:15 NIV).

I can pray a breath prayer, *Give me Your words,* when—

- a stranger asks me for money.

- my coworker is angry.

- a waitress is rude and impatient.

- I feel I'm being cheated.

- a hurting friend calls for advice.

**Give me Your words.**

# HELP ME BELIEVE.

*"Be not afraid, only believe."*

MARK 5:36 KJV

Who among us has never battled self-doubt?
Who can say they've never been afraid of
failing? Sometimes it seems the harder we try,
the more we mess things up. But God rewards
those who diligently seek Him, and overtakes
with abundant blessings those who put His
Kingdom first.

All He asks is that we acknowledge Him in
all we do; that we trust Him unwaveringly. He
loves us and cares for us watchfully, affectionately, and carefully. Faith works by love; and
God is eternally faithful, unchanging in His
determination to love you and show you His
infinite mercy. God is love. We are commanded
to walk in love and to love God with all our

heart, leaning not on our own understanding, but in all things, completely relying on Him. (See Proverbs 3:5.)

I can pray a breath prayer, *Help me believe,* when—

- I can't see a solution.

- circumstances seem to be spiraling out of control.

- I'm tired and at my wits end.

- others are angry and shouting.

- nothing seems to be working.

**Help me believe.**

# SHOW YOURSELF STRONG IN MY WEAKNESS, FATHER.

*"My grace is sufficient for you,*
*for my power is*
*made perfect in weakness."*

2 CORINTHIANS 12:9 NIV

We all feel incapable at times. Each of us has lacked the confidence we need to confront some challenge God has put in our path. Yes, God challenges us because He wants us to grow and mature by learning to rely on Him. He wants to demonstrate His strength through our weakness. If we're not challenged in our areas of weakness, how will we come to fully know God's strength?

Like David overcoming the lion and the bear, we are led into skirmishes and defensive battles

18

that test our courage more than our strength. David was the scrawny little brother who had the heart of a King. His heart was perfect before the Lord. Why? Because he relied on God's strength rather than his own. God tested his courage long before calling him to slay the giant. David experienced God's grace—by faith.

I can pray a breath prayer, *Show Yourself strong in my weakness, Father,* when—

- I've bitten off more than I can chew.

- I am given an opportunity I don't feel qualified for.

- my vision is bigger than my abilities.

- someone else is more experienced or well-known.

- I don't know what to do in a crisis.

**Show Yourself strong in my weakness, Father.**

# MAKE ME A BLESSING.

*Let us not be weary in well doing.*

GALATIANS 6:9 KJV

Most of us are much too busy to add anything more to our already overextended schedules. We cringe at the thought of additional obligations. We are ordinary people with limited time and finite abilities.

Yet all of us have experienced the exhilaration of being at just the right place at the right time to bless someone unexpectedly. Being "prepared for every good work" does not always require a financial investment or additional time commitment, but it always requires a willing heart.

The "preparation of the gospel of peace" spoken of in Ephesians is more of an attitude than it is a skill. Are we willing vessels, yielded to the leading and prompting of the Holy Spirit?

The joy of actually doing the gospel comes
from simply allowing God's love to be available
through us. To "be prepared" is simply to be
available, attentive, and mindful of those precious
moments when a spontaneous kindness can free
a soul to fly.

I can pray a breath prayer, *Make me a blessing,*
when—

- I need to be reminded about the power
  of God's love.

- I become preoccupied with my own
  problems.

- everyone around me is dwelling on the
  negative.

- I'm feeling selfish.

- I don't know what to do.

**Make me a blessing.**

# HELP ME CONTROL MY THOUGHTS.

*We take captive every thought to make it obedient to Christ.*

2 CORINTHIANS 10:5 NIV

Do your thoughts ever run away down a trail of offense? You might be singing praise songs in the car when suddenly you are cut off in traffic or slowed down by someone driving five miles under the speed limit. Angry exclamations race through your mind in an attempt to find their way out of your mouth. The joy of the Lord's presence evaporates and you struggle simply to hold your tongue.

But in Christ you are able to interrupt those "opposing thoughts" by taking a deep breath and reminding yourself of God's infinite mercy.

You can take every thought captive! Allowing patience to do its perfect work, you let the peace of God guard your heart and still your mind. You remember once again your hope of glory and allow the love of God to rule in that moment. His grace is always sufficient.

I can pray a breath prayer, *Help me control my thoughts,* when—

- I'm stuck in stop-and-go traffic.

- I'm picking up trash that a neighbor dog spread all over the yard.

- someone says something mean to me.

- I open the credit card bill after Christmas.

- my child knocks over their drink at a restaurant.

**Help me control my thoughts.**

# HELP ME TO TRUST IN YOU.

*Be still, and know that I am God.*

PSALM 46:10 NIV

It seems to be human nature to panic. Who doesn't expect the worst or try to keep expectations at a minimum? We all lay awake at night dwelling on the "what if's?" and the "how so's," and sometimes the "God help me's."

Often it is all we can do to remember that the steps of the righteous are ordered by God, that God is at work in every situation working out all for good on behalf of those who love Him. We need be anxious for nothing, knowing that God is always watching over us. We can let go of our concerns about how quickly we are reaching our destination and simply enjoy the journey.

24

If we are truly trusting in God, it is up to us to let go and let God carry us over life's rapids and rough places. Resting in Him can be the biggest challenge. Determine to let the peace of God rule in your heart, soul, and mind. Resolve to rest in God's perfect peace.

I can pray a breath prayer, *Help me to trust in You*, when—

- I can't sleep at night for worrying.

- I'm impatient and anxious.

- I'm bored.

- I don't understand.

- I want to know why.

**Help me to trust in You.**

# LORD, LET ME REST IN YOUR PEACE.

*Peace I leave with you,*
*my peace I give unto you: . . .*
*Let not your heart by troubled,*
*neither let it be afraid.*

JOHN 14:27 KJV

Pressed on all sides. Pulled in all directions. At times life seems to be reeling out of control. We want so much for circumstances to be predictable, our homes to be orderly, and our days to go as planned. When the kids get sick, the sink backs up, the car breaks down, and our boss makes unexpected demands, feelings of helpless exasperation can overwhelm even the bravest of us.

But we have an anchor in Christ. Although

the world around us seems to be falling apart, we know our steps are ordered by God. We can be at rest when the rest of the world isn't. We can cast our care on God knowing He is working out every detail for our good. We are command- ed not to be anxious but to allow the peace of God to reign in our hearts and minds—making every thought obedient to the gospel of peace— choosing peace, being at peace. Let God's peace work in you.

I can pray a breath prayer, *Lord, let me rest in your peace,* when—

- a deadline takes me by surprise.

- I can't remember where I left my keys.

- the dog next door won't stop barking.

- my child is late coming home.

- no one seems to care.

**Lord, let me rest in Your peace.**

# LORD, MAKE YOURSELF KNOWN.

*Your promises are backed by all the honor of your name.*

PSALM 138:2 NLT

Your unsaved friend is in the hospital under-going heart surgery. You send him an encouraging note including your heartfelt prayer for a smooth procedure and rapid recovery, and several scriptures telling of God's will to heal and deliver. You wait, hoping he has not only made it through surgery successfully, but also that he wasn't offended by your spiritual overtures.

God will make Himself known through each word you share. Release your concern, and allow the Holy Spirit to minister God's grace. God works through His Word. His Word is spirit and

life and will not return to Him void. You must
be ready to deliver it to those who inwardly seek
after the hope that is outwardly evident in you.
Lift up the word and let it go. Pray for God
to reveal himself, and know that it is through
His Word that He makes himself known in the
hearts of all men—including those you love.

I can pray a breath prayer, *Make Yourself known*,
when—

- my loved ones are suffering.

- I intercede for the unsaved.

- I pray for the sick.

- the world seems hopelessly ignorant.

- I am feeling weak.

**Make Yourself known.**

# MAKE ME FAITHFUL IN LITTLE THINGS.

*Whoever can be trusted with very little*
*can also be trusted with much.*

PSALM 71:21 TLB

Too much to do. So much to think about. So many distractions and urgent things demanding your attention. Small details often don't seem important compared to the weightier matters at hand. How we get to our destination does not seem as important as how fast we get there. And focusing on the minor details of how we conduct ourselves might require a major change in our lives. However, paying attention to the "means" —to how we make each step we take along the journey—can result in our consecration. And that consecration frees us from the world and makes us usable by God for bigger tasks.

Learn to care about every step of the process as much as the end product. We can practice a lifestyle of consecration by engaging more fully in the ordinary things we do. Dedicating all we do to the Lord and giving glory to God in all things requires that we do all things worshipfully, mindfully, thankfully, and joyfully. It's in the littlest things, the smallest details, that God observes our faith.

I can pray a breath prayer, *Make me faithful in little things*, when—

- rushing to get everything done.

- doing something I feel I shouldn't have to.

- no one is looking.

- big problems overwhelm me.

- I'm not getting paid.

**Make me faithful in little things.**

# GUARD MY HEART, FATHER.

*Above all else, guard your heart,
for it is the wellspring of life.*

PROVERBS 4:23 NIV

So much threatens to disturb our hearts. Every day we have to beat back the cares of this world that threaten to choke out the fruitfulness of God's truth at work in our lives. We may toil hard at sowing that truth in our heart—hearing and studying His word, contemplating and praying the truths we learn there—just to have God's enemy steal it away.

A farmer can put more effort into protecting his harvest than in sowing and reaping it. Although our willing hearts provide the rich soil for God's word to flourish—and His Kingdom to take root in our lives—we must be careful not to let the little foxes, birds, and thieves in this world trespass and destroy what God planted there.

We must guard our heart with all diligence because it is the source of our fruitfulness. Let the peace of God reign in your heart. May His love, peace, faith, hope, and joy rain continually on the fertile soil of your heart.

I can pray a breath prayer, *Guard my heart, Father,* when—

- the future seems bleak.

- I'm distracted or discouraged.

- circumstances are beyond my control.

- there is strife all around me.

- it's a challenge to be joyful or stay positive.

**Guard my heart, Father.**

# HELP ME KEEP IT SIMPLE.

*Whoever becomes simple and*
*elemental again, like this child, will*
*rank high in God's kingdom.*

MATTHEW 18:4 MSG

Too many of us have too much to think
about, function on too little sleep, don't have
enough time in the day, and suffer from sensory
overload. Demands for our attention seem to
increase as we speed into our futures. Even as
we are "liberated" by modern, time-saving
conveniences, we are at the same time oppressed
by higher expectations and greater demands to
achieve, have, and become more. The more
efficient we become, the more productive we
must be, right?

We seem to want more and more to compli-
cate our lives. Our thirsts can seem unquenchable.

But there is a Well that satisfies. Let's not forget the simplicity of the Gospel—the simple truth found in Christ. Christ the source of all peace, joy, and true contentment. Seek first the Kingdom of God and His Righteousness—seek first His rest. Seek the simplicity found in Christ.

I can pray a breath prayer, *Help me keep it simple,* when—

- I feel like I'm not achieving all I want to.

- I'm not satisfied with my life.

- I'm bored.

- I don't know how to rest.

- I can't seem to "keep up" with my neighbors or colleagues.

- I'm excited about a new project in my already busy life.

**Help me keep it simple.**

# GIVE ME YOUR
# WISDOM, LORD.

*Getting wisdom is the most
important thing you can do!*

PROVERBS 4:7 NLT

How can we know which way to go? How
can we be sure what to do? We are told to firmly
grasp the will of the Lord, not to be like the
foolish but like the wise—to be circumspect,
discerning, and prudent—to be led by the Spirit.

Without the wisdom of God, we can't know
truth. Without the living Word and Spirit at
work in our hearts and minds, we would not
have a clue about how to be righteous, walk in
love, or minister grace. We are able to partake of
God's divine nature, His excellence, and virtue
because His Word and Spirit live in us.

It's the love of God in us that brings us to the knowledge of truth, an understanding of holiness, humility, and honor. God has provided us with all things pertaining to life and godliness, including the very mind of Christ.

I can pray a breath prayer, *Give me Your wisdom, Lord,* when—

- my heart and mind don't agree.

- I am confused.

- I feel I'm not seeing the whole picture.

- there are great risks.

- I want to step out in faith without neglecting wisdom.

**Give me Your wisdom, Lord.**

# ORDER MY STEPS, LORD.

*The steps of the godly are directed by the Lord. He delights in every detail of their lives.*

PSALM 37:23 NLT

Circumstances press in, challenge our confidence, and force us to change course continually. People require our attention and test our affability. Sometimes we can't avoid the awkward situations we find ourselves in. Sometimes we are at a total loss about what to do. That's when we need to rest in the Lord, knowing the steps of a righteous person are ordered of God.

We can't ever fully understand the meaning of the events we experience unfolding before us. Often we have no idea where they are leading.

But God promises that He has our best interests at heart; He is watching over us carefully and affectionately. He is working out all things for our own good. We might not know what tomorrow will bring, but we can rest assured that God will be there to see us through. What a blessing to know our steps are ordered of God.

I can pray a breath prayer, *Order my steps, Lord,* when—

- I'm passed up for a promotion.

- my car breaks down on the highway.

- I'm running late.

- I find myself in an awkward situation.

- I don't understand why . . . .

**Order my steps, Lord.**

# COMFORT OTHERS
# THROUGH ME.

*Praise be to the God and Father of our
Lord Jesus Christ, the Father of compassion
and the God of all comfort, who comforts
us in all our troubles, so that we can
comfort those in any trouble with the comfort
we ourselves have received from God.*

2 CORINTHIANS 1:3-4 NIV

We comfort because we are comforted. We
serve the God of all comfort. If we are truly His
body in the earth, we are called to comfort the
sick, the brokenhearted, and the downtrodden.
What greater calling is there than to be a source
of comfort to a hurting world?

You might think that you're not a person
called to comfort the hurting and lost. But really,

it's not you alone that conveys comfort, but God's truth and Spirit working through you that bring about the comforting. All we must do is speak it, hold it up, draw attention to it, and the love and mercy of God does the comforting for us. God's Word is always comforting. You are just the vessel God uses to carry His comfort to the hurting.

I can pray a breath prayer, *Comfort others through me,* when—

- I see hurting and despair.

- I feel incapable of helping.

- I can't find the words.

- no one else is taking the lead.

- those around me are overwhelmed.

**Comfort others through me.**

# HELP ME USE MY TIME WISELY.

*Make the most of every opportunity
for doing good in these evil days.*

EPHESIANS 5:16 NLT

Time is our most precious, non-renewable resource. It's so easy to take it for granted and easier still to squander it. It takes enormous effort to harness and direct it. However, the returns can be equally enormous if we invest it well. We must rely on the Holy Spirit to prompt us how best to use those 'disposable' moments we are given.

What is it that takes up much of your leisure time? Have you fallen into a pattern that keeps you from accomplishing the things that are in your heart to do? There is nothing wrong with wholesome entertainment and recreation. But distractions that seem harmless can become subtle time traps that cause us to neglect the dream God has placed in our hearts, or neglect reaching out to someone in need.

Throughout the New Testament, we are urged to be diligent and disciplined with how we use the little time we have been given. Are we "spending" our time foolishly or "investing" it wisely?

I can pray a breath prayer, *Help me use my time wisely,* when—

- I find I have some extra time.

- I need to spend time with you, Lord.

- I'm in between commitments.

- too many demands pull me in different directions.

- I'm tempted to sleep instead of pray.

**Help me use my time wisely.**

# DRAW ME CLOSER TO YOU, LORD.

*As the deer pants for streams of water,*
*so my soul pants for you, O God.*

PSALM 42:1 NIV

*I love you, Lord,* you think to yourself on your way to work—remembering you didn't get up to seek His presence, or maybe didn't even pray before going to sleep. You want more of God in your life, more of His presence, a more intimate relationship with the Holy Spirit. After all, how can you be sensitive to the leading and prompting of the Lord's Spirit if you haven't spent any time with Him?

Many of us love the Lord with our whole heart; we really do. We love to worship Him on Sunday and listen to His word preached from the pulpit. But we have trouble living in His presence the other days of the week. Maybe we spend a few minutes acknowledging the Lord on some days, a brief conversation here and there, but never really manage to sit at His feet daily.

As your heart cries out throughout day, "Draw me closer to you, Lord"—as you lie on your bed at night with that longing in your heart, He will surely draw you to Him.

I can pray a breath prayer, *Draw me closer to you, Lord,* when—

- my life seems out of balance.

- I'm stressed.

- too many distractions vie for my attention.

- others make me feel inadequate.

- I need hope.

- I've lost my joy.

- I need to make time for You.

**Draw me closer to you, Lord.**

# GUIDE OUR LEADERS, LORD.

*First of all, then, I urge that entreaties and prayers, petitions and thanksgivings, be made on behalf of all men, for kings and all who are in authority, so that we may lead a tranquil and quiet life in all godliness and dignity.*

1 TIMOTHY 2:1-2 NASB

Listen to the news. Read the papers. Hear what people are saying. Most reports about our elected leaders are critical and negative. It doesn't take long to recognize the difficult position in which many of our public officials find themselves, especially as viewpoints grow diverse and naysayers become louder. We know that the loudest voices are not necessarily the wisest and that it is impossible to please everyone.

Pray for our leaders. Pray that moral clarity and excellence will govern our elected leaders. As small interest groups become more vocal, pray that principle takes precedence over popularity. In today's media-driven political campaigns, pray that character is valued more than charisma. Today more than ever, we must pray for our political system and its leaders.

I can pray a breath prayer, *Guide our leaders,* when—

- they are struggling with decisions in foreign policy.
- fear and confusion blind us to justice and truth.
- moral clarity is confused by complexity.
- Christian leadership faces strong opposition.
- the country becomes trapped in sin and dishonesty.

**Guide our leaders.**

# YOU ARE FAITHFUL, FATHER.

*If we are not faithful,
he remains faithful, because he
cannot be false to himself.*

2 TIMOTHY 2:13 TEV

Our hearts are heavy with the burdens and cares of this world. Yet when we go to the Lord with our needs, a little voice prattles on in the background about how we have reaped what we've sown, taken God's goodness for granted, fallen short in what we've been called to do, or failed to pull our weight in the Kingdom. We can each think of a dozen reasons why we don't deserve God's blessing.

Giving what is not deserved, loving unreservedly, and being unconditionally, is the very nature of God's grace. God offers salvation to the sinner, strength to the weak, sight to the blind—yet none deserve it. Though we can never earn God's blessing, we know His grace and mercy are always greater than our shortcomings. God is faithful.

Pray a breath prayer, *You are faithful, Father,* when—

- I'm not sure if You hear my prayers.

- my life seems to be falling apart.

- others are not being faithful.

- I don't feel worthy.

- my kids are going astray.

- my checking account is empty.

**You are faithful, Father.**

# HELP ME REMEMBER.

*When the Father sends the Counselor as
my representative—and by the Counselor
I mean the Holy Spirit—he will teach
you everything and will remind you of
everything I myself have told you.*

JOHN 14:26 NLT

People are forgetful by nature. History
repeats itself. Sometimes conversations are called
"scripts" because they are used over and over.
We are told to renew our minds, that faith comes
by hearing and hearing again, and that the Holy
Spirit will bring all things to remembrance. If we
weren't forgetful beings, why would the Bible
tell us this?

Sometimes it seems we'll never get it right.
Our intentions are good, our plans are sound—
we can organize and strategize—but then com-

50

pletely forget what we set out to do. We are creatures of habit, of convenience, and though we mean well, we don't always remember what it was we meant to do long enough to follow through. We intend to call, or write, or send a donation, or pray—but we just forget!

One of the enemy's primary techniques is to keep you so busy that you forget what God has put on your heart to do. Write down your vision, just in case you forget.

I can pray a breath prayer, *Help me remember,* when—

- my family is demanding my attention.
- plans change unexpectedly.
- I'm running from one thing to the next.
- I can't stay focused.
- things "come up."
- I'm trying to do too many things at once.

**Help me remember.**

# Forgive me, Lord.

*He is faithful and just to*
*forgive us our sins.*

1 John 1:9 kjv

It's the little foxes that spoil the vine. We've all heard Solomon's expression. Perhaps we've stretched the truth a bit, lost our temper, or watched something we shouldn't have on TV. It's the little things that cause us to stumble, the seemingly harmless temptations that come between us and walking in fellowship with God.

When we do turn to God in prayer, we are convicted of our sins. Deep within ourselves we know we haven't walked uprightly before God—we've not been holy even as He is holy—with singleness of heart, pursuing first the kingdom of God and His righteousness. The Lord compels us to put away the entanglements that so easily grab and hold us, those habits that keep us from continually walking in His Presence. (See Hebrews 12:1). But we are also assured that He is faithful to forgive all our trespasses if we but ask.

I can pray a breath prayer, *Forgive me, Lord,* when—

- I don't use my time wisely.

- I haven't sought you first.

- I spoke negatively about another.

- I bought something I didn't really need.

- I saw someone in need and looked the other way.

- I've watched shows that polluted my thought life.

**Forgive me, Lord.**

# MEET MY NEED, LORD.

*My God shall supply all your need
according to his riches in glory
by Christ Jesus.*

PHILIPPIANS 4:19 KJV

Rising prices. Increasing bills. Worsening
debt. Unexpected costs, or even expected ones,
can end up being more than we can pay. Add to
that the needs of others in our communities,
schools, churches, and institutions as funding is
cut and budgets are stretched. We are being
asked to give increasingly more as individuals to
support public programs and local schools.

There have been certain years when we have
felt more strongly the effects of our nation's
struggling economy. Most of us will certainly
face financial challenges of some sort in the
future. Natural circumstances might not offer

much hope, but God himself promises to meet our needs. He calls himself Jehovah Jireh—the God who provides—in the Old Testament. And in the New Testament we are told that all our needs are met according to His riches in glory. In uncertain times, it is good to have a certain word about God's will to meet our need.

I can pray a breath prayer, *Meet my need, Lord*, when—

- income is uncertain.

- gas and utility prices skyrocket.

- extra costs spring up by surprise.

- there seems to be no way to make ends meet.

- I've pledged to give more than I have.

- the cars and our teeth need repair.

**Meet my need, Lord.**

# KEEP ME FROM STUMBLING.

*Lead us not into temptation,
but deliver us from evil.*

MATTHEW 6:13 KJV

As Christians, we are called to be leaders and examples. We are called to be capable teachers and mentors. But we are also human beings daily battling temptations to watch too much TV, eat or drink things we know aren't good for us, or say things we shouldn't. Who among us doesn't struggle to stay on track?

Sometimes all we can do is admit our weakness, lean on God to help us through those momentary temptations to turn on the TV, lose our temper, or keep our eyes from gazing longingly at a doughnut until we can no longer resist its allure. Being mindful of the Lord's leading can keep us from getting carried off by worldly distractions, and continually seeking His presence will cause us to stumble less frequently. The surest way to keep from falling down is to lean on God.

I can pray a breath prayer, *Keep me from stumbling,* when—

- I'm too tired to resist.

- my flesh wants to indulge itself.

- everyone around me is doing it.

- I'm looking for any excuse to procrastinate.

- people-pleasing takes precedence over purpose.

**Keep me from stumbling.**

# YOU ARE MY STRENGTH, ALMIGHTY FATHER.

*The LORD is the strength of my life.*

PSALM 27:1 KJV

From the moment we open our eyes each morning until we close them again at night we must remind ourselves that the challenge is not what we can do for the Lord but what the Lord can do through us. There is so much to be done, so many people to reach, so many needs to meet. Sometimes we are asked to undertake a worthy objective, but feel inadequate to achieve it.

Thankfully, our hope is not in our personal abilities. We don't need to bear the burden of saving the world single-handedly. Our strength comes from the Lord, and we are only one part of a great body fulfilling God's purpose in the earth. God not only promises to show himself strong where we are weak, but He will also give us the measure of faith we need to trust Him. The biggest challenge is learning not to rely on our own limited knowledge and personal strengths, but to rely on God's wisdom and strength working in us.

I can pray a breath prayer, *You are my strength, Almighty Father,* when—

- I'm asked to do something I've never done.

- my natural self wants to run and hide.

- my emotions are taking over.

- my buttons are being pushed.

- I feel inadequate and afraid.

- I'm worn out and the day isn't over.

**You are my strength, Almighty Father.**

# SHIELD ME WITH YOUR FAVOR, LORD.

*For surely, O Lord, you bless
the righteous; you surround them with
your favor as with a shield.*

PSALM 5:12 NIV

The situation seems impossible. Time has run out. You might be hoping against all odds for a visa to travel or waiting nervously to get through customs. There could be a language barrier or a legal barrier keeping you from your goal. Perhaps you are waiting to hear back about an audition or a job interview. Or maybe you're just standing in the customer service line, hoping to exchange a disappointing gift.

You are usually just one person or one conversation away from your answer. To be shielded by the favor of God is to receive the grace you need at a time when you need it most. Pray, believing that God's favor is surrounding you like a shield, and each hopeless situation is a platform for the miraculous. Tap into the favor of God simply by trusting in it.

I can pray a breath prayer, *Shield me with Your favor, Lord*, when—

- no one seems to want to help me.

- I need paperwork approved.

- I'm waiting for a response from my lawyer.

- I'm up for a promotion.

- I need to close a deal.

**Shield me with Your favor, Lord.**

# I PRAISE YOU, HOLY AND AWESOME GOD!

*O Lord, I will praise thee . . . Praise the
Lord, call upon his name, declare
his doings among the people, make mention
that his name is exalted.*

ISAIAH 12:1,4 KJV

God's goodness is overwhelming. His faithfulness is mind-boggling. His mercies are
astounding. What can we do but praise Him?
As we drive in our cars, sit at our desks, or stand
at our kitchen sinks, we are in awe of God's
goodness and faithfulness to each and every one
of us. He has not forgotten a single one of us;
He even knows the number of hairs on each of
our heads!

Sometimes all we can do is offer praise in

return for the Lord's awesome goodness and faithfulness. All we can offer in return for His mercy and kindness is our heartfelt thanks. All He wants from us is our willingness to see Him as He is, which will lead to our adoration and gratitude. What more can we do but offer thanks and exalt His name? God is worthy, holy, and just. He is majestic and mighty to be praised! Praise the Lord today.

I can pray a breath prayer, *I praise You, holy and awesome God*, when—

- I wake up in the morning.

- I'm on my way to work.

- I'm waiting for the time to pass.

- I'm on my way home.

- I lay down to go to sleep.

**I praise You, holy and awesome God!**

# MAKE ME AWARE OF YOUR PERSPECTIVE, FATHER.

*For by the grace given me I say to every one of you: Do not think of yourself more highly than you ought, but rather think of yourself with sober judgment, in accordance with the measure of faith God has given you.*

ROMANS 12:3 NIV

Days turn into weeks—weeks into months—and months into years. We hardly notice the change that takes place in ourselves as time passes by. Are we growing? Are we being transformed into the person God designed us to be? How do our lifestyles and habits measure up? Have we stepped back and taken stock of how far we have come on our spiritual journey?

Perspective is the process of not only recognizing where we are in relation to where we are going but also how we measure up to Christ, the hope of glory in us. In his letter to the Ephesians, Paul urges us to be circumspect. That means being self-aware, to see ourselves objectively, to judge ourselves. Many of us are too busy to stop and consider ourselves deeply. Take an opportunity for that deep rest and reflection. Remember to take time to reflect and be mindful.

I can pray a breath prayer, *Make me aware of Your perspective, Father,* when—

- my priorities are out of place.

- weeks go by without rest.

- something always takes precedence over quiet time.

- I'm irritable because I'm feeling disconnected.

- I need to stop and think.

**Make me aware of Your perspective, Father.**

# TEACH ME HOW TO PRAY.

*Lord, teach us to pray.*

LUKE 11:1 KJV

When we come to the Lord in prayer, we often wonder if we're approaching the throne acceptably. It may seem cavalier the way we talk to God as if He were our best friend, or come running to the throne of grace at any hour unannounced. We come as we are—dirty, dusty, tired, or hurting—we come when we're excited, expectant, frustrated, or angry. We come running like children—messy, transparent, and trusting.

Jesus related several parables about the nature of prayer in Luke eleven. He described prayer as a type of knocking and seeking that demands a response. Even the man who is asleep in bed will rise to answer the door, if only to appease the knocker. But we are also shown that if we ask bread of our Father in heaven, will He who loves us give us a stone? It's not a matter of how we come to the Father in prayer, but that we come.

I can pray a breath prayer, *Teach me to pray,* when—

- I'm not sure what to say.

- my children are sick.

- my problem seems overwhelming.

- someone needs a touch from you.

- it's early and I'm sleepy, but I want to seek you first.

- I'm discouraged.

**Teach me to pray.**

# I'M HERE TO LISTEN, FATHER.

*He wakens My ear to hear as a disciple. . . .*
*The Lord God has opened My ear, and I*
*have not been rebellious or turned backward.*

ISAIAH 50:4 AMP

Early in the morning we rise to pray. Half asleep we may call upon the name of the Lord. We offer praise and thanksgiving. We make our requests known. We pray in the Spirit. But do we listen? Do we know how to hear the still, small voice of the Lord in those quiet times, or do we fill our prayer time with a running monologue of all our problems, desires, and requests?

Learning how to listen during times of prayer is as important as knowing how to whole-heartedly exalt Him and boldly come before Him with our needs. We have been taught in our culture to state our opinion, make demands, boldly ask, and claim what is ours while the skills of waiting, listening, and hearing have become a lost art. Cultivate the ability to sit and listen—not only to others, but also to the Lord. Hear what the Spirit is saying. Be patient, be still, and listen.

I can pray a breath prayer, *I'm here to listen, Father,* when—

- I'm panicking.

- others need guidance.

- I want to spend quality time with You.

- I don't know what else to say.

- You have something for me to do.

- I need You.

**I'm here to listen, Father.**

# YOUR JOY, LORD, IS MY STRENGTH

*"Do not be grieved, for the joy of the Lord is your strength."*

NEHEMIAH 8:10 NASB

What more can you do after you've done everything? You've prayed, believed, confessed God's promises, and stood strong. What more can you do to exercise your faith during a difficult situation? The circumstances don't seem to be changing. You feel stuck in the mire of your problem with your light of hope rapidly dimming and your faith weakening.

In the midst of a crisis, the last thing you feel like doing is rejoicing. But perhaps joy is like a bucket that we can use to draw answers from the wells of salvation. We are literally commanded to rejoice throughout the Old and New Testaments regardless of our circumstances. Reach deep within yourself to tap into the deposit of joy God placed in your heart. When you came to the Lord He put His joy, peace, and love there. That is the source of your strength. Renew your strength by rejoicing.

I can pray a breath prayer, *Your joy, Lord, is my strength*, when—

- all seems lost.

- I have done everything I know to do.

- negative circumstances are over-whelming me.

- others are talking badly about me.

- I have been offended and hurt.

**Your joy, Lord, is my strength.**

# BE MY CONFIDENCE, LORD.

*So do not throw away your confidence;
it will be richly rewarded.*

HEBREWS 10:35 NIV

An opportunity arises for you to pray with a stranger. They have a need; you know the Answer. Their eyes are on you; they are waiting. What hope do you have to offer them? Never before have the fields been as ripe for harvest. Will you labor with the Lord to bring light to a dark place?

We don't lack for opportunities to share Christ, but we often lack confidence. Peter lacked confidence, but was transformed from a cowering follower to one of the boldest leaders in church history. Paul asked his readers to pray for his boldness to increase. Paul prayed that his disciples would have confidence in Christ and the boldness required to share the Gospel. Throughout the New Testament, we are encouraged to grow in confidence and boldness as we share our testimony. Ask the Lord to give you confidence to reach out with His love today—even if only in a small way.

I can pray a breath prayer, *Be my confidence, Lord,* when—

- I have an opportunity to pray for someone.

- I'm asked to do something outside my comfort zone.

- my kids are challenging my position.

- I'm not sure if I'm on the right track.

- I'm speaking in public.

**Be my confidence, Lord.**

# HELP ME TO PERSEVERE.

*Renew a right, persevering, and steadfast spirit within me.*

PSALM 51:10 AMP

The winter grows long. The days drag on. We go through seasons of putting out seemingly endless fires. God must have timed the seasons so they test our ability to persevere—just when we can't take one more day of the summer heat, the autumn wind, the winter chill, or the spring rain, a new season begins.

When the seasons grow long, or the daily grind seems unbearable, we lean on the Lord for strength to keep going. Isaiah tells us that those who hope in the Lord "shall change and renew their strength and power; they shall lift their wings and mount up as eagles [mount up to the sun]; they shall run and not be weary, they shall walk and not faint or become tired" (Isaiah 40:31 AMP). We should not become weary in doing good. Be assured that God always helps us to endure when we lean on Him.

I can pray a breath prayer, *Help me to persevere,* when—

- work gets more and more stressful.

- my child's teacher asks me to be homeroom parent.

- the kids are trying my nerves.

- I'm completely out of ideas.

- I'm shoveling snow while it's still snowing.

- the bills keep coming.

**Help me to persevere.**

# HEAL ME.

*Heal me, O LORD, and
I shall be healed.*

JEREMIAH 17:14 KJV

Ugh . . . you feel awful. Your head throbs, your muscles ache, and you feel weak. How can you do all you're supposed to today? You wonder if you should call in sick and cancel all your appointments. You wonder, "Can I ask God to heal me?"

Yes, you can. James 5:14-15 invites the church to pray for their sick. This passage also promises inner healing along with physical healing. Jesus himself welcomed individuals to approach Him with their request for healing. You can come to Him today. God told the Israelites that He is "The Lord, who heals you" (Exodus 15:26 NIV). And Peter quoted Isaiah,

76

saying by Jesus' wounds we were healed. (See Isaiah 53:5 and 1 Peter 2:24.) Take heart, believe what the Bible says, and ask God to heal you.

I can pray a breath prayer, *Heal me,* when—

- I'm not feeling well.

- the doctors give me a negative report.

- my heart is broken.

- despair threatens to overwhelm me.

- I don't understand the cause of my symptoms.

- I have a headache and am ready to take some aspirin.

- nothing else is working.

**Heal me.**

# BLESS THE WORK
# OF MY HANDS.

*The Lord shall command a blessing on . . .*
*everything you put your hand to.*

DEUTERONOMY 28:8 NIV

When we set out to work each day, we never know exactly how the Lord will use us. Even as we perform the most mundane tasks, we can bring a measure of excellence and grace to everything we set our hand to. Even as we undertake the most challenging responsibilities, we can lean on God for special insight, skill, and courage.

Most of us would admit that without God's grace we wouldn't have the patience required to do those tedious jobs like folding laundry, filing reports, or balancing our checkbooks. And without God's grace, we would never have made that deadline or succeeded in delivering such a winning presentation. As believers, we can start each day assured that God is with us, prospering all we set our hands to. If we are acknowledging the Lord in all we do, trusting in Him, and not leaning on our own understanding, we will not be ashamed or disappointed—the Lord will bless our work.

I can pray a breath prayer, *Bless the work of my hands,* when—

- I have a huge responsibility to fulfill.

- I am tempted to procrastinate out of fear or dread.

- I am asked to do something that is beyond my ability.

- I'm lacking confidence.

- I'm running behind.

**Bless the work of my hands.**

# HELP ME REST IN YOUR LOVE.

*This is my commandment, That ye love one another, as I have loved you.*

JOHN 15:12 KJV

These three remain: faith, hope, and love. But the greatest of these is love (1 Corinthians 13:13).

If we could walk in the love of God all of the time, we wouldn't be afraid. Why? There is no fear in love. (See 1 John 4:18.) When we are convinced that we are truly safe in God's love, that His will really is the best thing for us, and that He will never fail to meet our needs; we stop being afraid. Along with that fear, greedy and prideful thoughts fall by the wayside. We are certain deep down inside that we are safe, no matter what circumstances surround us. Sound like a peaceful, happy life? You bet it is. So begin building a life where you feel safe all the time, and pray that you will be convinced of the depths of God's love for you.

I can pray a breath prayer, *Help me rest in Your love,* when—

- my patience is being tested.

- others are critical of me.

- too many demands are made on my time.

- I am frustrated.

- I don't think I'm being treated fairly.

- my energy begins to fail.

**Help me rest in Your love.**

# GROW YOUR PATIENCE IN ME, JESUS.

*Let patience have her perfect work, that ye may be perfect and entire, wanting nothing.*

JAMES 1:4 KJV

Most of us spend our days rushing from one task to the next. We talk fast, walk fast, and expect fast service, fast cash, and fast credit. Red lights don't turn green fast enough. Our meals must be ready instantly. Things just don't happen quickly enough. We grind our teeth while on hold, waiting in line, or waiting for a Web page to download—we hate to wait.

If we continue to move through life in a state of perpetual haste, we will sacrifice opportunities to hear the Holy Spirit speak. Growth

82

and maturity become evident as we exercise this discipline. In addition, an abundance of patience is required to be a good listener, counselor, or teacher who purposefully nurtures and cultivates others. Patience is a fruit developed by God's presence in you. Let God begin to work His own patience into your life.

I can pray a breath prayer, *Grow Your patience in me, Jesus,* when—

- it seems there is no time.

- there is always something else that needs my attention.

- people fumble or talk slowly.

- someone else's problem doesn't seem important.

- I'm waiting in line.

**Grow Your patience in me, Jesus.**

# MAKE ME THE PARENT YOU ARE, FATHER.

*"If you then, being evil, know how to give good gifts to your children, how much more will your Father who is in heaven give what is good to those who ask Him!"*

MATTHEW 7:11 NASB

As parents, we often ask ourselves whether we are doing everything possible to cultivate our children's God-given gifts and talents. There are so many choices to make about what is best for them, so many decisions about how best to raise them for the glory of God.

We are blessed with easy access to the Bible through a variety of translations. We can worship freely, preach, teach, and proclaim our faith openly. Christian schools, youth ministries, and even Christian radio stations abound. We do not lack for Christian opportunities for our children in the wider community, but is Christianity lived out in our homes? How do we conduct ourselves privately? Are we "walking the talk" in our homes?

We can enroll our kids in Christian schools and send them to the best Christian camps—but what are they learning as they watch us?

I can pray a breath prayer, *Make me the parent You are, Father,* when—

- my children's needs don't align with my personal agenda.

- I'm upset with my spouse.

- I can't give them what they want.

- they have questions about tough social issues.

- school is hard.

- I've lost my patience.

  **Make me the parent You are, Father.**

# MAKE YOUR WILL KNOWN AND I WILL FOLLOW.

*The steps of the godly are
directed by the Lord. He delights
in every detail of their lives.*

PSALM 37:23 NLT

Oh, to know God's heart! If we could only be sure of God's perfect will in every situation. But sometimes it seems to elude us. We want to be faithful and sensitive to the leading of the Holy Spirit at all times. Praying, seeking, sometimes fasting, we often struggle to know which way to go, what path to follow, or exactly how to proceed.

We are told in John 10:4 that we were given the ability to discern the Lord's voice and follow

His leading when we devoted our lives to Him. We can know God's will to the extent that we get to know Him. Press in, seek His Presence, purpose to know the Lord intimately, and you will not feel confused, alone, or aimless. You can know the heart of God, and there you will discover the peace of assurance.

I can pray a breath prayer, *Make Your will known and I will follow,* when—

- prioritizing my time.

- I don't know how much to give or to whom.

- more than one way seems right.

- my heart and my head don't agree.

- my spouse and I don't agree.

**Make Your will known and I will follow.**

# I CAST ALL MY CARE ON YOU.

*Casting the whole of your care . . .*
*on Him, for He cares for you affectionately*
*and cares about you watchfully.*

1 PETER 5:7 AMP

More money, a better marriage, stronger
medicine. Improved health, increased wealth,
greater wisdom. So much weighs on our minds.
What if the day we finally pay our debts our
health fails, or we become physically fit and
financially secure just to lose our marriage. We
all make mistakes; we all stumble and fail at
times. But those who run to the Lord will find
mercy and grace in their time of need. They will
find their answer hidden in God.

We can look to doctors, bankers, counselors,

and experts for answers. But those who put their trust in the Lord will never be forsaken or ashamed. God is faithful even when we're not. Test Him, prove Him, make your need known to Him today. He waits patiently and mercifully for you to place your hope in Him once and for all. He is the God that provides all the answers and meets all your needs. He is your solution.

I can pray a breath prayer, *I cast all my care on You,* when—

- my problems get out of hand.

- I'm in the middle of managing a crisis.

- there is too little of me to go around.

- I don't know what to do.

- my life seems to be falling apart.

**I cast all my care on You.**

# RENEW MY YOUTH.

*Who satisfies your mouth [your necessity
and desire at your personal age and situation]
with good so that your youth, renewed, is
like the eagle's [strong, overcoming, soaring]!*

PSALM 103:5 AMP

No matter what age we are, we feel as if life
is passing by too fast. We may feel we're "old"
at thirty or forty, fifty or sixty. Or we don't
"feel" old at all, but wonder how those wrinkles
got so deep. We look at our lives, frustrated that
we haven't been able to do more. What happened
to those dreams that got put on hold?

Young people are full of expectation. Their
futures are wide open, and the whole world seems
to be theirs for the taking. They start new schools,
jobs, or projects with excitement and anticipation.
Why should parents and grandparents be any less

expectant? As parents our priorities naturally change from pursuing our own personal passions to helping our children discover and pursue theirs. But God has not withdrawn His special dream for you. Renew your youth by reviving your dream. Stir up those latent desires tucked away in your heart. All things are possible with God!

I can pray a breath prayer, *Renew my youth*, when—

- it seems I missed my chance.

- I'm feeling discontent and disinterested in my life.

- I don't feel useful anymore.

- I've lost my sense of fun and adventure.

- I lack a sense of purpose.

**Renew my youth.**

# DELIVER ME, LORD!

*And call upon me in the
day of trouble: I will deliver thee,
and thou shalt glorify me.*

PSALM 50:15 KJV

Oppression comes in many forms. A job or town we don't like, a family situation or financial obligation that has us in its grip. We can feel captive to a variety of things all at the same time. There may seem to be no way out—no way of escape.

We all go through seasons of captivity. We have all experienced a "wilderness time" of confusion and fear. But God always delivers those who fully rely on Him. He always rewards the faithful with freedom. Fear not; only believe. Hang on to the Lord, He will see you through your rough spot and promote you, lifting you up and out in due time. You are never alone, never forsaken. God is with you. He will deliver you.

I can pray a breath prayer, *Deliver me, Lord!* when—

- I feel trapped in my job.

- financial burdens are more than I can handle.

- I feel hemmed in by my circumstances.

- I need a break.

- I find myself in a dangerous situation.

- people are putting pressure on me.

**Deliver me, Lord!**

# HELP ME TO HEAR YOUR VOICE.

*You will give me greater honor than before
and turn again and comfort me.*

PSALM 71:21 TLB

The loud voices of the world yell out for our attention. The little voices in our head are whispering their opinion. Choruses of voices pull us in every direction. None of us lack for a choice of voices to listen to. The challenge is focusing on the right voice. Which voice will you heed? Which of all those voices will you engage in conversation? Which will you allow to speak into your life?

There is but one voice that we must follow —the voice of our Heavenly Father. Recognizing the Father's voice shouldn't be difficult if we know the Father. How easy it is to distinguish the voice of our earthly father who calls out to us from a crowd of people. It's a comforting, protective voice of authority that you trust and recognize. God wants nothing more than for you to know, hear, trust, and follow His voice.

I can pray a breath prayer, *Help me to hear Your voice,* when—

- there seem to be too many voices vying for my attention.

- I'm seeking Your perfect will in a given situation.

- I don't know what to say.

- several good opportunities present themselves.

- following my heart means taking great risks.

- I need wisdom, not advice.

**Help me to hear Your voice.**

# HELP ME BE MORE CONSISTENT.

*Therefore return to your God!*
*Hold fast to love and mercy, to righteousness*
*and justice, and wait [expectantly]*
*for your God continually!*

HOSEA 12:6 AMP

Consistency. Some of us stay the course most of the time, but most of us only some of the time. Some days we get it right, some days we stumble a lot. Some days we might take time to pray but neglect an opportunity to give. And it's the little inconsistencies that really bring us down and wear us out. Maybe we'd grow less weary in well-doing if we were more consistent in doing well.

The Lord is consistent. The Bible tells us that

the Lord is with us continually, that He guides us continually. God asks us to be steadfast, continuing daily in the faith. We are to set His commandments continually before us, not just sometimes. (See Proverbs 6:21.) This is also our hope because in doing so we will have continual success.

We can continually hope in Him even as David did when he proclaimed, "I have set the Lord continually before me; because He is at my right hand, I shall not be moved" (Psalm 16:8 AMP).

I can pray a breath prayer, *Help me be more consistent,* when—

- I'm tempted to slip back into bad habits.
- I know what to do but don't always do it.
- self-discipline is a challenge.
- disciplining my children.
- people are relying on me to set an example.

**Help me be more consistent.**

# KEEP THEM SAFE.

*He ordered his angels to guard you
wherever you go. If you stumble, they'll catch
you; their job is to keep you from falling.*

PSALM 91:11-12 MSG

There they go. You watch your children get
on the bus. You wave goodbye as your spouse
drives off. You call after them "Be careful!" as
they walk down the street on their way to school
or a friend's house. You release them to the care
of the Lord as they get on the plane. There seems
little you can do once they are out of sight.

As you attempt to put your concern for
them out of your mind, you breathe a prayer:
"Keep my children safe, Lord." You pray that
God's angels would encamp around them and
that the Holy Spirit would direct their steps to
safety; that they would be blessed in their going

and coming. What a comfort to know that God hears our prayers and that His Word does not return to Him void. (See Isaiah 55:11.)

I can pray a breath prayer, *Keep them safe, Lord,* when—

- my children go off to school.

- my spouse goes on a business trip.

- my parents go on vacation.

- friends or family are in the military.

- the youth group goes on mission trip.

- close friends move overseas.

**Keep them safe, Lord.**

# MAKE ME A BETTER FRIEND.

*There is a friend that sticks
closer than a brother.*

PROVERBS 18:24 NKJV

It's easy to take friends for granted—especially good friends. When we are busy, tired, or stressed, we might withdraw to ourselves and neglect to let our friends know how important they are to us, how much we care for them and appreciate them. They have always been there for us during times of crisis; but do we give back as we take?

Being a good friend takes effort. We must be careful to invest in our friendships. We are told in John 15:13 that there is no greater love than to lay down our life for a friend. Jesus said we would be counted as friends if we continued doing what He asked us to do. God called Abraham His friend because Abraham believed in Him. When was the last time you let your friends know that you believed in them? That you loved and appreciated them and would lay down your life for them?

I can pray a breath prayer, *Make me a better friend, Lord,* when—

- I get caught up in my own problems.

- I forget to keep in touch.

- I need to send an encouraging word to a struggling friend.

- there is a special kindness for which to be thankful.

- a new neighbor needs a friend.

**Make me a better friend.**

# HELP ME WALK HUMBLY BEFORE YOU, LORD.

*And what doth the Lord require of thee,*
*but to do justly, and to love mercy,*
*and to walk humbly with thy God?*

MICAH 6:8 KJV

For those of us raised in church understanding God's covenant promises and the authority we have in Christ comes naturally and it is easy to fall prey to spiritual arrogance. We might take God's goodness for granted; His sweet fellowship might become overly familiar. We might consider His blessings a right rather than a privilege. We lose sight of the sacred, forget to esteem the holy, and often lack reverence when we come boldly to the throne of grace.

Yes, we are God's beloved children; He is

our affectionate Father. But we are also told that the fear of God is the beginning of wisdom. Micah reminds us what the Lord really requires of us is to love mercy, do justice, and walk humbly before God. Yes, God's mercies are new every morning and His lovingkindness never ends. Yet, we must also remember to walk reverently before the Lord, worshipfully, and humbly, not lightly esteeming the sacrifice He made for our redemption. Holy is the Lord.

I can pray a breath prayer, *Help me walk humbly before You, Lord,* when—

- I open my mouth to speak.

- I come to You in prayer.

- I'm tempted to do something I know would grieve You.

- I sit down to eat.

- I lightly esteem the mercies of God.

**Help me walk humbly before You, Lord.**

# MAKE ME A VESSEL OF HONOR.

*As the clay is in the potter's hand,*
*so are you in my hand.*

JEREMIAH 18:6 NKJV

*Vessel* can refer to any type of container. It's a word that seemed to have had much more significance in ancient cultures. In antiquity, clay pots were very important, perhaps like saucepans or sealed plastic containers today. They were the primary instrument used to cook, store, or transfer food or water. If a pot was cracked or weak, it caused many problems.

Throughout the Bible, God uses the illustration of clay pots, or vessels, to describe the role of nations and individuals. In Jeremiah, God says that as clay is in the potter's hand, so are we in

His hand. David cries out in Psalm 31:12 (AMP), "Like a broken vessel am I." Hosea condemns Israel as being among nations of useless vessels. We are called "vessels of mercy" in Romans 9:23 (NKJV) and are told in 2 Corinthians 4:7 that we possess the precious treasure of the gospel in earthen vessels. We are also instructed in 2 Timothy 2:21 to separate ourselves from all wrongdoing that we might be vessels of honor fit for the Master's use and prepared for every good work.

I can pray a breath prayer, *Make me a vessel of honor,* when—

- I want to be used in ministry.

- I want to be an example to my children.

- I am in a position of leadership in my community.

- determining how to give.

- setting goals for the future.

**Make me a vessel of honor.**

# THANK YOU FOR THIS DAY, LORD.

*This is the day the Lord has made;*
*We will rejoice and be glad in it.*

PSALM 118:24 NKJV

The sun is shining. The birds are singing. It's another beautiful day. God's creation is a testimony to His goodness and majesty. The beauty of each dawn is an illustration of God's new mercies every morning—each vibrant sunset His faithfulness. Rejoice and be glad for the heavens and the earth belong to the Lord. Through Him all things were made; without Him nothing was made that has been made. (See John 1:3 and Hebrews 11:3.)

There is much to thank the Lord for every day—the air we breathe, the water we drink,

and the abundance of food and friendship.
Most of us have enough to eat and a warm place
to sleep, and we can go about our towns and
neighborhoods in relative peace. Yes, there is a
time to mourn and repent, a time to make our
needs known to God, to cast our cares in faith,
a time to intercede, and a time to pray for peace.
But we must not neglect gladness and thanksgiving—for this is the day the Lord has made.

I can pray a breath prayer, *Thank You for this
day, Lord,* when—

- showering in the morning.

- driving to work.

- running errands.

- watching my children at play.

- walking my dog.

- ending the day.

**Thank You for this day, Lord.**

# KEEP ME ON YOUR PATH, LORD.

*We can make our plans, but the LORD determines our steps.*

PROVERBS 16:9 NLT

You head out into your day full of purpose, determined to check everything off your to-do list. You pray as you go, asking the Lord to help you to do it all. Things come up throughout the day—fires need fighting, crises need managing, friends call seeking advice—and the next thing you know you've been derailed. Or have you?

Sometimes God had goals for us that needed to go to the top of our list. That friend, that fire we put out—maybe those were things He had for us to do. Yes, God has called us to be steady, purpose-driven people, and He has given us the spirit of power, love, and a sound mind—a calm, well-balanced mind, disciplined and self-controlled. (See 2 Tim 1:7.) Yes, we can do all things through Christ. In fact, we are told we have the very mind of Christ! (See 1 Corinthians 2:16.) And that is the key. Staying on God's track for your life might involve tasks that don't appear on your list. Keep checking in with Him.

I can pray a breath prayer, *Keep me on Your path, Lord,* when—

- I'm having trouble meeting my commitments.

- other's needs seem to take precedence over my own.

- there is more to do than there is time.

- I have a pressing deadline.

- I'm having trouble prioritizing.

**Keep me on Your path, Lord.**

# HELP ME SPEAK THE TRUTH IN LOVE.

*But speaking the truth in love, [we] may grow up into Him in all things.*

EPHESIANS 4:15 KJV

Poor communication, or the complete lack of it, is undoubtedly the cause of most misunderstandings and unhappiness. Speaking the truth can be difficult. Expressing ourselves honestly and openly is a huge challenge that we all must work at throughout our lives. Seasoned with love, however, honest communication can liberate, heal, and nurture our relationships.

The Bible has a lot to say about communication. Speak the truth in love—be ready always to give an answer for the hope that is in you. A kind word, a gentle tongue, and a disciplined mouth are incredible forces for good. James tells us, "If any man offend not in word, the same is a perfect man, and able also to bridle the whole body" (James 3:2 KJV). Let the love of God not only constrain your words, but also compel you to speak the truth in every situation.

I can pray a breath prayer, *Help me speak the truth in love,* when—

- reasoning with my spouse.

- confronting a coworker.

- disciplining my children.

- speaking up in a church group.

- standing for what is right in my community.

- I want to deceive myself about something.

**Help me speak the truth in love.**

# GUIDE ME IN MY GIVING.

*Each man should give, . . .*
*not reluctantly or under compulsion,*
*for God loves a cheerful giver.*

2 CORINTHIANS 9:7 NIV

How can we be sure when and how much to give? After all, our resources are limited. Our own needs feel so great that it's hard to think about the needs of others. How can we possibly feed the hungry, shelter the homeless, care for the widows, and clothe the naked? And giving your coat away to whoever asks for it seems a little extreme when you have a family to provide for.

Our minds have difficulty grasping that whatever good deed we do will be rewarded by the Lord—that anytime we give things or blessings in any way, it is regarded by God as if we've done the same thing to Him. What if the stranger that asks for a nickel was Christ himself? What if the poor in the Third World was Jesus crying out for our attention? Have we left Christ in some prison? Have we neglected Him by neglecting the needy? Let God show you what to do.

I can pray a breath prayer, *Guide me in my giving*, when—

- strangers ask for money.

- I see pictures of starving children in Third World countries.

- my church asks people to get involved in prison ministry.

- someone in my congregation has a need.

- resources are limited, but my compassion knows no bounds.

- I feel overwhelmed by the requests in my mailbox.

**Guide me in my giving.**

# WAKE ME UP!

*He wakens me morning by morning.*

ISAIAH 50:4 NIV

"Wake me up, Lord! Please don't let me roll over and go back to sleep. Help me seek You early in the morning. I want more of You, but I usually choose to sleep. Help me to hear You calling me to spend time with you. Keep me from being sleepy and lax when I have an opportunity to fellowship with You. Let me give You my complete, undivided attention . . ."

This is the heart cry of many of us. We intend to wake early and pray more. We intend to be fully engaged whenever we spend time with God. But we either can't get out of bed until the last minute, or when we find a free moment, we turn on the TV. We can go through our whole lives as if we're sleepwalking. We might pray, but only be half there.

"Wake up, O sleeper, rise from the dead, and Christ will shine on you! Be very careful, then, how you live—not as unwise but as wise, making the most of every opportunity" (Ephesians 5:14-16 NIV).

I can pray a breath prayer, *Wake me up, Lord,* when—

- I need to get up early and pray.

- I don't give You my full attention.

- I'm going through my day as if You weren't there.

- I need to be aware of what You are saying.

- I have an opportunity to do something eternal for You.

- You just want to spend time with me.

**Wake me up!**

# WHERE IS IT, LORD?

*There is nothing covered that
will not be revealed, and hidden
that will not be known.*

MATTHEW 10:26 NKJV

Is there anything more frustrating than not
being able to find what you're looking for? You
search and search and can't find it anywhere. It's
enough to drive you crazy. A gamut of emotions
overtakes you from frustration, to anger, to panic,
to grief—finally, when all else fails, you meekly
ask the Lord to help you find it . . . you put
aside your vain attempts to tear through closets
and drawers and humble yourself in prayer.

You ask the Holy Spirit to please reveal
where this thing is hidden—you let it go and
choose peace, putting it momentarily out of your
mind. If it's something you need right away, you

calmly relax, turn your attention inward, and prayerfully yield yourself to follow wherever the Holy Spirit prompts you to look. You feel prompted to look again somewhere you may have searched already—and there it is!

I can pray a breath prayer, *Where is it, Lord?* when—

- I can't find my car keys.

- my kids can't find their homework, and they're late.

- I can't find my glasses.

- I haven't seen something for awhile and now wonder where it is.

- I just saw something and now can't recall where.

- a friend is upset over a missing item.

**Where is it, Lord?**

# HEAL MY BROKEN HEART.

*The Lord is close to the brokenhearted and saves those who are crushed in spirit.*

PSALM 34:19 NIV

So many things tear at our hearts. Regrets, disappointments, lost opportunities. Because we love deeply, we grieve deeply with any loss. It seems the more we share of ourselves, the more we expose our vulnerabilities. We want to give love and trust, but perhaps our heart still smarts from a past wrong.

Jesus came to heal the broken hearted. Isaiah declared that God will revive the heart bruised with sorrow. (See Isaiah 57:15 AMP.) God will grant consolation and joy to those who mourn—

to give them an ornament of beauty instead of ashes, the oil of joy instead of mourning, and the garment of praise instead of a heavy, burdened, and failing spirit—that they may be called oaks of righteousness, the planting of the Lord, and that He may be glorified. (See Isaiah 61:3 AMP.)

This is why He came: To restore our joy that our joy might bring Him glory.

I can pray a breath prayer, *Heal my broken heart*, when—

- I've been hurt in a relationship.

- disappointment overwhelms me.

- a deal goes bad.

- I miss out on an opportunity.

- I lose something or someone I love.

- I just hurt inside.

**Heal my broken heart.**

# GRANT ME SOUND SLEEP.

*When you lie down,
your sleep will be sweet.*

PROVERBS 3:24 NIV

It's midnight. You've been lying in your bed for two hours waiting for sleep to overtake you. You intended to get up early and pray, exercise, or maybe write in your journal. These good intentions led you to turn in early, yet here you are wide awake another hour later at 1:00 a.m. You count sheep, the things on your to-do list, the hours left before morning.

Your thoughts cry out, *Lord, how will I get up early to seek You if I can't go to sleep?* When you are too tired to get up and pray, remind yourself that "he gives his beloved sleep,"

120

and "I will lie down and sleep in peace." (See Psalm 127:2 NKJV and Psalm 4:8 NIV.) You can relax. The Lord is with you. He will grant you sound sleep and sweet dreams. Rest in His peace and fall safely asleep.

I can pray a breath prayer, *Grant me sound sleep*, when—

- my mind won't quiet down.

- I'm tired but can't get to sleep.

- I'm anxious.

- noises keep me awake.

- my kids pile in bed with me.

- tomorrow is going to be a high-pressure day.

**Grant me sound sleep.**

# MAY I BE QUICK TO FORGIVE.

*Forgive, and ye shall be forgiven.*

LUKE 6:37 KJV

Forgiveness can be the most challenging yet powerful tool we have in our spiritual tool belt. Being quick to forgive is like turbo-charging that tool. Over time, we usually "get over it," completely forget, or manage to get an offense off our chest in one way or another. We can then say that we have forgiven the "past" wrong— but by then forgiveness is long overdue. We must learn to forgive in the present moment.

Being quick to forgive requires that we forgive as soon as the opportunity to get offended presents itself—that we don't embrace the offense in the first place. Don't reach for it, but deal with it before it can roost in your mind and build a wall of offense. The best way to keep hurts from planting themselves like weeds in your soul is to be quick to forgive. Forgiveness is the weed-eater of your mind. The ultimate power tool to clear a path to the fullness of God's grace and mercy.

I can pray a breath prayer, *May I be quick to forgive,* when—

- someone is rude to me on the phone.

- my spouse says something hurtful.

- people speak negatively about me.

- the nice things I do go unnoticed.

- I feel cheated.

**May I be quick to forgive.**

# OPEN MY HEART TO YOUR PLAN FOR MY LIFE.

*For I know the thoughts and plans that
I have for you, says the Lord.*

JEREMIAH 29:11 AMP

Most of us have wondered about our unique purpose ever since we were very young. Who are we in this world? Were we born at a particular time and place for a reason—with our own particular set of gifts and talents? These are the questions most of us have churning around in the back of our minds. Are we moving closer to—or farther away from—God's plan for our lives? Can we know it?

"I know the plans I have for you," the Lord told Jeremiah. And His plan is that we seek Him with all our heart, and the Lord will make himself known to us. (See Jeremiah 29:11-14.) We know that when we seek God with our whole hearts the Lord directs our steps. "And we know that all things work together for good to them that love God, to them who are the called according to His purpose" (Romans 8:28 KJV). Seek first God's heart and purpose, and there you will find your own.

I can pray a breath prayer, *Open my heart to Your plan for my life*, when—

- I lack direction.

- the work I do seems meaningless.

- I don't know which way to go.

- I need to prioritize my commitments.

- I need more money but want to continue doing what I feel called to do.

- I wonder if I have been following my own plan instead of Yours.

**Open my heart to Your plan for my life.**

# MAKE ME YOUR
# PEACEMAKER, LORD.

*Blessed are the peacemakers: for they shall
be called the children of God.*

MATTHEW 5:9 KJV

Tension. Hostility. Envy. Strife. The climate
is heavy and oppressive. Negative feelings expand
like clouds to fill the atmosphere. You feel a
sense of hopeless frustration as communication
breaks down and solutions seem nowhere in
sight. You want to smooth things over but don't
know how.

Your heart longs for peace. You pray for just
the right words to bring light to this dark situation. Nothing seems worth losing God's peace
over—certainly not "every evil thing" that strife
will usher in (James 3:16 NASB). You purpose to

make peace. You find that peace is the desire of
your heart—and those desires are God-given.
He will fulfill that desire by making you a
minister of His grace. Speak words of peace, and
you will see the strongholds of contention come
crashing down.

I can pray a breath prayer, *Make me Your
peacemaker, Lord,* when—

- my children are fighting.

- there are disputes in my church.

- I have friends who don't get along.

- there are rivalries where I work.

- there are arguments between teams
  in my recreational league.

**Make me Your peacemaker, Lord.**

# RENEW MY MIND, HOLY SPIRIT.

*Be transformed by the renewing of your mind.*

ROMANS 12:2 NIV

Self-imposed limitations. Preconditioned thinking. Limited perceptions. We've all heard how our thoughts determine our life experience and level of success. Visualization and positive thinking can be powerful forces while negative mindsets and destructive thought patterns limit us. We are told in Romans 12:2 to be transformed by the renewing of our minds—but what exactly does that mean?

Ephesians 4:23-25 (AMP) tells us to "be constantly renewed in the spirit of our mind [having a fresh mental and spiritual attitude], and put on the new nature . . . created in God's image,

[Godlike] in true righteousness and holiness." That seems to be a tall order. But we have been given all things pertaining to life and godliness so that we can do just that. (See 2 Peter 1:4.) Put on the mind of Christ by reading and meditating on the Word daily. There is no surer way to renew the mind, be transformed, and become the success you long to be.

I can pray a breath prayer, *Renew my mind, Holy Spirit,* when—

- I feel I'm not worthy or lack confidence.

- I need a fresh perspective.

- I can't seem to communicate with my child.

- I don't know how to pray for a situation.

- I need to understand someone better.

- I'm anxious.

**Renew my mind, Holy Spirit.**

# RESTORE MY HONOR.

*You will give me greater
honor than before and turn
again and comfort me.*

PSALM 71:21 TLB

Scorned. Humiliated. Laughed at. Ridiculed.
Have you ever been in a situation where others
looked upon you with disdain? It could be the
result of some failure on your part, the color
of your skin, or because you have been abused.
Or perhaps you have been falsely accused of
something. Any of these situations would cause
you to hang your head in shame.

But this is not the stature of a child of God.
This is not the end of your story. No situation is
beyond the help of God. He will cleanse you if
you need cleansing. He will restore your reputation. He honors you and places great value on

you because you are His child. He loves you and surrounds you with His favor as a shield. Instead of being bowed down, stand up and hold your head high. You are a child of the King!

I can pray a breath prayer, *Restore my honor*, when—

- others look down on me.

- I am ashamed of myself.

- my reputation has been destroyed.

- I have failed You.

- I have been rejected.

**Restore my honor.**

# PROTECT ME FROM TEMPTATION.

*Lead us not into temptation,
but deliver us from evil.*

MATTHEW 6:13 KJV

Temptation. It comes in many forms, seemingly out of nowhere. We don't intend or desire to be tempted. We make every effort to avoid temptations of all sorts—temptations to overindulge, get angry, speak negatively, or waste time—or any number of bad habits we've struggled to overcome. The list can be endless.

The thing you've tried most to avoid is the one thing that you stumble across time and again. If it's doughnuts, all of a sudden coworkers are bringing you doughnuts. Strength of will doesn't always provide the answer, but prayer does. Jesus taught his disciples when praying to not only ask for daily provision, but also for protection from temptation. Ask the Lord to keep temptation far from you, to clear your path of the stones that might cause you to stumble.

I can pray a breath prayer, *Protect me from temptation,* when—

- I commute to work.

- I enter the office.

- I am headed to meet with someone who rubs me the wrong way.

- I'm on my way to a restaurant to meet friends for lunch.

- I leave for home in the afternoon.

- thoughts come into my mind that I don't want to give in to.

**Protect me from temptation.**

# MAKE ME FAITHFUL.

*Who then is that faithful and
wise steward, whom his lord shall
make ruler over his household?*

LUKE 12:42 KJV

Jesus taught many parables on the significance
of stewardship. In addition to servant leadership,
it is one of the primary principles we must take
hold of as Christians. We are called to reach out to
the lost, prefer one another in love, be examples
of righteousness, and to grow in our faith. But
we don't often hear about taking care of what
we already have—our bodies, our finances, our
families, our careers. We might pay careful
attention to one area just to neglect another.

Being a faithful steward is akin to being a
faithful servant. It is in going about our daily
responsibilities with inward faithfulness, but this

attitude also becomes an outward expression as we take care of our homes, cars, physical bodies, personal appearance, and so on. Taking care of such things is like tending a garden. We are called to keep them well. How are you keeping the garden God has given you?

I can pray a breath prayer, *Make me faithful*, when—

- My money doesn't go far enough.

- I don't have enough time.

- I finally purchase something I've wanted for a long time.

- I don't have time to talk with my spouse or family.

- I have several hours of unscheduled time.

- I receive a beautiful gift.

**Make me faithful.**

# GIVE ME A WILLING HEART.

*If you willingly obey me, the best crops in the land will be yours.*

ISAIAH 1:19 CEV

Many things cause us to harden our hearts. It can be a mood we're in or a prejudice we have. Our own circumstances might cause us to become bitter or to feel that we are not in a position to serve. Daily we are presented with opportunities to be a blessing to someone. Often we are not even aware of those cues—we are asleep in our own concerns.

Ephesians 5:14 calls sleepers to awake and rise from the dead. We are told that in so doing Christ would give us light in order that we might live purposefully and accurately—we are urged to make the most of every opportunity, submitting ourselves one to another in reverence for Christ. (See Ephesians 5:15-20.) In verse 9 of the same chapter it tells us that the "fruit of the Light consists in every form of kindly goodness, uprightness of heart, and trueness of life" (AMP). Showing kindness and mercy is how we turn our hearts upward, rather than inward. An "upright heart" is a willing heart.

I can pray a breath prayer, *Give me a willing heart,* when—

- I don't want to do what I know I should.

- I am having a tough time at work.

- someone asks for help.

- I am going through a difficult time at home.

- I deal with obstinate people.

- I feel like I can't get out of bed.

**Give me a willing heart.**

# SPEAK THROUGH ME.

*Do not worry about how or what
you should speak; for it will be given you
in that hour what you should speak.*

MATTHEW 10:19 NKJV

What an honor it is to be used to voice the heart of God. Not only do we want our words to be pleasing to God and bring encouragement to others, but we want also to teach and preach with authority, even to prophesy. These are gifts with which God has equipped the Church to edify herself. We are called as Christians to be examples, mentors, and teachers. God urges us to study the Word and to accurately handle the word of truth, preparing ourselves to give an answer to anyone who asks. (See 2 Timothy 2:15 and 1 Peter 3:15.)

Look for occasions to share the hope you

have in Christ and to shine the light of the
Gospel on a world bound in oppression to sin.
Share the knowledge you have of the Truth that
sets free—for "how beautiful are the feet of
those that bring good news" (Romans 10:15).
Look around you; the fields are ripe for harvest.
Go and make disciples (which means "students")
of all those around you for faith comes by
hearing—and how will they hear if there is no
teacher? (See Romans 10:14,17.)

I can pray a breath prayer, *Speak through me*,
when—

- I see people in need.

- my child feels hurt or confused.

- I am part of a team.

- I find myself leading.

- people around me feud.

- I feel You nudging me to say something.

**Speak through me.**

# BE MY ROCK, GOD.

*The Lord is my rock, my fortress
and my deliverer; my God is my rock,
in whom I take refuge.*

PSALM 18:2 NIV

There are times when you might feel like
you are being swallowed up by quicksand. Your
emotions are overwhelming, threatening to drag
you under. Or perhaps things are changing so
rapidly around you that you need something
solid to grab onto.

Have you ever heard the phrase, "hard as a
rock" or heard of a person referred to as "the rock
of Gibraltar"? Well, God wants to be your rock.
Tougher than the hardest diamond and unmoved
by any circumstance, He stands firm and solid,
Someone you can hold onto. Or if you just need
to take a break and rest awhile, He is there for

you as a rock of refuge, protected from the storms of life as you shelter inside His strength.

I can pray a breath prayer, *Be my rock, God,* when—

- I need to stand strong.

- the winds of change are changing everything around me.

- I have failed.

- I need someone to hold onto.

- I need a break from my circumstances.

**Be my rock, God.**

# GRANT ME YOUR WISDOM AND CREATIVITY, LORD.

*I, wisdom, dwell with prudence, and find out knowledge of witty inventions.*

PROVERBS 8:12 KJV

No clue. Nothing. Blank. You sit and stare into space. And that's all it seems there is between your ears—empty space. The only thing you are able to fill the space with is a cry to God for a fresh idea, divine inspiration, or brilliant insight. And of course, God's throne room is the best place to go.

When you're out of ideas, go to God. He is the Master Creator who created you in His image. He has given you the ability to imagine and innovate—the power to come up with witty inventions. There is no well too dry, no mind too stale for God to fill with inspiration and creativity. When you need a new approach or a fresh perspective, ask God. He is the Great Revealer of profound, deep, and ever astounding revelation. Does God in all His Infinite Wisdom have any special insights or fresh ideas for you? Why don't you ask Him?

I can pray a breath prayer, *Grant me Your wisdom and creativity, Lord,* when—

- I feel like I am beating my head against the wall.

- there is something I don't understand.

- I need to show my spouse love.

- my work seems monotonous.

- I am on the planning committee for an event.

**Grant me Your wisdom and creativity, Lord.**

# THANK YOU FOR YOUR MERCY.

*It is of the Lord's mercies that we are not consumed, because his compassions fail not. They are new every morning: great is thy faithfulness.*

LAMENTATIONS 3:22-23 KJV

How many times throughout the course of the week do we stumble and regret something we've said or done? We run to God for forgiveness while at the same time a voice inside our head tells us that we're not worthy, not good enough, and completely unable to walk in God's will. Why should we even try? It seems sometimes we'll never get it right. Why should God continue to forgive us time and time again?

Perhaps this is why God assures us over and over of His mercy. He tells us His mercies are new every morning; they never come to an end. He proves His faithfulness by always responding to our repentance with forgiveness. (See 1 John 1:9.) God wants our hearts more than our good works. In Psalm 51:17 (AMP), we are reminded that "[the sacrifice acceptable] to God is a broken spirit; a broken and a contrite heart [broken down with sorrow for sin and humbly and thoroughly penitent], such, O God, You will not despise."

I can pray a breath prayer, *Thank You for Your mercy, Lord*, when—

- I neglected to do something.

- I've continued to do something I said I would no longer do.

- I forget to put You first.

- I turn away from the needy.

- I'm irritable and impatient.

- I awake and realize it is good to be alive.

**Thank You for Your mercy, Lord.**

# PREPARE ME FOR EVERY GOOD WORK.

*And God is able to make all grace
abound toward you; that ye,
always having all sufficiency in all things,
may abound to every good work.*

2 CORINTHIANS 9:8 KJV

We've all been told that preparation is the ultimate key to success. We know that champions are those who are better prepared than their opponents. Victories are won through training and preparation. And there is no better way to take advantage of opportunities that come your way than to be prepared for them.

Paul tells Timothy, "Who separates himself from contact with contaminating and corrupting influences] will . . . be fit and ready for any good

146

work" (2 Timothy 2:21 AMP). Preparation
requires self-discipline. As a soldier preparing for
war, or an athlete for competition, we must set
ourselves apart and press forward. (See
Philippians 3:14.) How do we do that? Through
studying the Word of Truth that transforms us.
There is no better preparation than being firmly
grounded on the foundation of the Truth.

I can pray a breath prayer, *Prepare me for every
good work,* when—

- I am waiting for a breakthrough.

- I'm seeking my calling and purpose.

- I am making plans for the future.

- I'm setting priorities and managing
  my time.

- spending time with my children.

- nothing is happening, and I'm tempted
  to let down my guard.

**Prepare me for every good work.**

# YOU ARE MY HOPE, LORD.

*Why are you downcast, O my soul?*
*Why so disturbed within me?*
*Put your hope in God, for I will yet*
*praise him, my Savior.*

PSALM 42:5 NIV

Hopelessness. You can see it in the faces of so many people. Maybe you see it in your own face today as you look in the mirror. Perhaps you are facing a crisis, and all of the facts say that it's all over, so you might as well give up. Or you are facing a situation that has been going on for so long that you have become weary and no longer see any reason to be hopeful? Does there appear to be no way out? Have you lost all hope?

Well, if that describes you, there's good news.

There is always hope with God. Even when the circumstances say otherwise, you can hope because God can and does work miracles. Your situation may be beyond human help; but God is your hope, and He is working on your behalf. Jesus said, "All things are possible with God" (Mark 10:27 NIV). So go ahead and pray in hope.

I can pray a breath prayer, *You are my hope, Lord,* when—

- I see no way out.

- my emotions are spiraling downward.

- I can't do anything to change my situation.

- I need a miracle.

- all appears lost.

- I don't know what to do.

**You are my hope, Lord.**

# I LOVE YOU, LORD.

*Love the Lord your God with all your
heart and with all your soul and with all your
mind and with all your strength.*

MARK 12:30 NIV

"I love you." These three precious words
never fall on deaf ears. It's the most heavenly
sound a parent can hear from their child—and
the sweetest sacrifice we can offer our Heavenly
Father. Yet sometimes it's difficult to find the
right words to tell our Savior how much we love
Him. But when all other words fail, these three
words are enough.

We can demonstrate love in many different
ways—through giving, good deeds, acts of
kindness, encouraging words. We can praise the
Lord through singing, dancing, and clapping our
hands or by approaching Him reverently in

worship—bowing low or raising our hands. But of all the ways we show God our adoration, nothing is sweeter than the spontaneous utterance of "I love You, Lord" any time throughout the day. Don't forget to remind the Lord how much you love Him today.

I can pray a breath prayer, *I love You, Lord,* when—

- driving in my car.

- sitting at my desk.

- working in the kitchen.

- exercising.

- lying in my bed.

**I love You, Lord.**

# BLESS MY LOVED ONES.

*I looked for someone to stand up
for me against all this, to repair the defenses
of the city, to take a stand for me
and stand in the gap to protect this land so
I wouldn't have to destroy it.*

EZEKIEL 22:30 MSG

Our hearts go out to those we love. When
they hurt, we hurt. We want to offer them our
strength and give them courage—but we also
want them to grow and mature in Christ. God
must feel the same way toward those He loves.
He already made the ultimate sacrifice by taking
our sin upon himself at the Cross. He paid a high
price that we might be counted righteous and
therefore inherit all the blessings He promised to
His covenant people. But we must learn to trust
in Him.

Interceding for those we love, holding them up before the Lord and covering them in prayer, is the best help we can offer. Empathy, advice, and all sorts of good intentions don't compare to the power of prayer. Laying down your life or making great personal sacrifice might be heroic, but not necessarily effective. The most trustworthy and loving thing we can do as Christians is to stand in the gap through prayer for those we love—just as Christ stood in the gap for us.

I can pray a breath prayer, *Bless my loved ones,* when—

- they are going through a difficult time.

- their situation seems hopeless.

- they need a touch from You.

- they need to feel Your presence.

- they are away from home.

**Bless my loved ones.**

# HELP ME OVERCOME EVIL WITH GOOD.

*Love your enemies, do good to them which hate you, bless them that curse you, and pray for them which despitefully use you.*

LUKE 6:27-28 KJV

There are some people that just know how to push your buttons. Or worse, they might really mean to do you harm. People might think or speak negatively about you, or unintentionally offend you. Maybe circumstances just don't seem to be working out in your favor. We want to take control so things will work out for our benefit— or we are tempted to justify ourselves at any cost.

It seems no matter what the situation, love is always the right answer. Proverbs tells us "a soft answer turns away wrath" and "a merry heart does good like a medicine" (Proverbs 15:1 NKJV and Proverbs 17:22 NKJV). Our joy and peace and gentleness can often bring healing to people or situations around us like a much-needed dose of antibiotic. Love, often displayed through patience, is a powerful anecdote. After all, it's the goodness of God that brings repentance. (See Romans 2:4.) We often underestimate the transforming power of mercy—think how God's grace and mercy has transformed you.

I can pray a breath prayer, *Help me overcome evil with good,* when—

- someone is bullying my child.

- people around me have selfish motives.

- I loose faith in my leaders.

- I want to strike out at someone.

- I have a conflict with one of my children's teachers.

**Help me overcome evil with good.**

# TAKE AWAY MY SHAME.

*There is now no condemnation for
those who are in Christ Jesus.*

ROMANS 8:1 NIV

Sometimes those who oppose us want nothing
more than to cause us shame. They point their
finger, place blame, give haughty looks, and
speak in ways that make you feel inferior.
Likewise, our spiritual enemy has been called
the "accuser of the brethren" because his main
objective is to make sure we feel guilty, unworthy and condemned (Revelations 12:10 KJV).
He keeps us down by attempting to erode our
self-image.

The New Testament is full of illustrations
describing the changes Christ has brought about
in us. We are new creatures, forgiven, made
righteous, beloved children of God, more than

conquerors, kings, priests, a holy nation. We have been called to glory and virtue. James likens the Bible to a mirror in which we see a reflection of how God sees us in Christ. (See James 1:23). Allow God's mercy to restore you, His grace to refresh you, and press on toward the high calling of God in Christ Jesus.

I can pray a breath prayer, *Take away my shame,* when—

- I regret something I've said or done.

- I feel foolish and unworthy.

- others look down on me.

- I feel guilty about my past.

- I'm embarrassed.

**Take away my shame.**

# HELP ME BELIEVE
# THE BEST.

*Love . . . is ever ready to believe the best.*
1 CORINTHIANS 13:7 AMP

The human mind seems to focus on the negative. We troubleshoot, criticize, and disapprove. We are all critics. We hope our criticism is constructive—we mean to bring about positive change through pinpointing problems and shortcomings everywhere we find them. But sometimes magnifying the negative does just the opposite.

God's wisdom and grace directs us toward a different approach. In Philippians 4:4-8 we are told to always rejoice, be anxious for nothing, but in everything by prayer with thanksgiving make our requests known unto God, and the peace of God will guard our hearts and minds.

Finally, we are told to only think on whatever is true, pure, lovely, admirable, excellent, or praise-worthy. We are to be ever ready to believe the best of every person, remain hopeful under all circumstances. (See 1 Corinthians 13:7 AMP.) Decide to focus on what's going right.

I can pray a breath prayer, *Help me believe the best,* when—

- coworkers aren't performing to my standard.

- the project isn't going as well as I think it should.

- I'm losing patience.

- a situation seems ridiculous.

- I can't understand why something must be done a certain way.

- accusations and rumors are flying.

**Help me believe the best.**

Additional copies of this and other
titles from Honor Books are available
from your local bookseller.

*Breath Prayers for African Americans*
*Breath Prayers for Mothers*
*Breath Prayers for Women*

If you have enjoyed this book,
or if it has had an impact on your life,
we would like to hear from you.

Please contact us at:

HONOR BOOKS
Cook Communications Ministries, Dept. 201
4050 Lee Vance View
Colorado Springs, CO 80918
Or visit our Web site:
www.cookministries.com